Roger Abrantes

Dogs
Home Alone

Wakan Tanka Publishers
1999

Published by Wakan Tanka Publishers, Naperville, Illinois, USA
Printed by Distinctive Printing & Graphics, Naperville, Illinois

1st edition 1999

Typeset in Times 11 pt at Lupus Forlag. Printed and bound in the USA.

Table of Contents

About this book 6

Foreword 7

1. Dogs home alone 9
2. Don't do this! 15
3. The treatment of CHAP 21
4. The dog learns to be alone 29
5. The daily routine 37
PS – Psychopharmacology 41
6. Bongo home alone 44

Index 46
Litterature 47

About this book

The various icons show what type of chapter you are about to read and what kind of exercises, including difficulty level, you are about to learn how to execute.

The book icon means that the chapter is a theoretic one including necessary information in order to execute the practical exercises successfully.

The dog icon shows that the text in question gives information as how to execute practical exercises correctly. There are easy and difficult exercises. For each exercise a difficulty level is accessed.

The stairs icon tells how difficult an exercise is, the easiest being at level 1. Exercises at a lower level must be performed satisfactorily before moving on to a higher level of difficulty.

Bongo is the reader's little helper. He gives useful tips throughout the book.

These fields, resembling the common command buttons on many computer programs, indicate signals to dogs. They always have two words connected by a comma without a space. The first word, beginning with a capital letter, refers to the meaning of the signal. The second word after the comma shows the form of the signal, e.g. a sound or a body movement.

! indicates a positive reinforcement and the word between "" indicates the specific reinforcement, e.g. a treat or the word good. The icon to the left shows that we must reinforce the dog's behavior with the word *good* and the icon to the right that we must give the dog a treat.

This icon means that the reader is welcome to get free on-line help from the author of this book, at the phone number +45 70201919, or by E-mail at roger@abrantes.com.

Foreword

Home alone is the canine behavior problem that we have treated with greatest success in the Etologisk Institute. We have through the years modified the original program, which we began working on nearly 20 years ago. The idea is still the same—to teach the dog, slowly but safely, how to be home alone. We tried to sweeten the transition from being together with mother and siblings 24-hour a day to suddenly being left alone in an unknown environment. We have to understand that it is highly unusual and unnatural for a dog, not to mention a little puppy, to be alone.

We have modified the original program throughout the years according to our increasing number of experiences and the very beneficial reports we got back from the dog owners. On various occasions, we have undertaken controlled experiments of new programs or parts of programs. The result of our work can be read in this book.

There is no perfect program to treat behavior problems in animals. Animals are individuals as different from one another as we humans are different from our conspecifics. We cannot therefore expect any standard program to achieve the same effect on all animals.

The program described in this book is a standard program. Some dog owners will experience that their dogs learn to be home alone inasmuch as they follow the program in all its details. Others will experience improvements and still others will only observe small changes.

The ideal is to adapt this standard program to the single dog. The reader is welcome to contact us at the Etologisk Institute where in most cases we will be able to adjust the original program to the reader's dog so we can reach satisfying results.

Start reading this book from one end to the other to gather an impression of the main idea of this book. Then carry out the exercises systematically one after the other. It is a good idea to practice the exercises at first without the dog for the owner to train the timing of signals and reinforcements.

Readers can also advantageously use this book to prevent the problem from showing up. Many dogs first show severe symptoms of not being able to be home alone when their puppy time is over. Sometimes we can yet solve the problems, but we have wasted valuable time. I cannot repeat it too often: prevention is better than cure.

Start with the exercises described in this book from the very first day the puppy enters your home. The puppy will then grow up as a strong dog, self-confident and with the ability to deal with unexpected situations.

Thanks to the staff of the Etologisk Institute for all help with the experiments and treatments of several thousand dogs that we have examined and to whom we have designed programs. A special thanks to examined animal behaviour therapist Susan Viegaard, pictured in this book with the dog Thais, for ideas and comments.

Solbjerg, Denmark 1997

I have slightly edited and enlarged the present English edition of this book. There is a new chapter about psychopharmacology since serious studies have been conducted intensively in this field in the last years. In spite of the slight different conditions for dog owners and dogs in Europe and in the U.S., many American dog owners have applied the program described in this book to their dogs. They have been as successful as their European counterparts. I wish to thank the American pet behaviorists who have tried my ideas, especially Sandy Myers from Narnia Pet Behavior, Naperville, IL and Pia Silvani from St. Huberts, Madison, NJ.

Buford, Wyoming 1999

Roger Abrantes

8

1. Dogs home alone
—The causes of the problem

It is not natural for dogs to be home alone. They would not be alone if they lived in their original surroundings. The dog has, as a pack hunter, a strong genetic disposition to feel comfortable in the company of others, primarily conspecifics, but also humans to whom they are imprinted very early in their lives— and to detest being alone.

Dogs are the descents of the wolf, a highly social animal. A wolf is never alone from birth to death. It is not natural for our dogs to be home alone and they have to learn it before they can cope with that situation.

"My dog cannot be home alone"—the most common SOS we hear at the Institute of Ethology in Høng, Denmark; and we have heard it a lot, since we began researching animal behaviour and helping animal owners and their animals in the last 15 years.

It is up to the dog owner to decide how important the problem is. Sometimes the dog is so destructive

Puppies and young dogs—up to one year old—learn to be home alone, under normal circunstances, after 14 days of training.

that the owner is compelled to get rid of it—and not so seldom to have the dog euthanized.

Statistics show that we can solve 95 percent of all problems provided we treat them before the dog is one year old. The older the dog, the more difficult it is to solve canine home alone problems (CHAP). CHAP is the name I prefer to give this very common canine problem, instead of canine separation anxiety, since, as you will see, it is very seldom that dogs suffer from a real separation anxiety. As you also will see, there are many reasons for dogs not being able to be home alone.

We have an overall success rate of 87 percent in our treatment of dogs with CHAP, independently of the age of the dog.

There are good chances to teach the dog to be home alone and the earlier you start the better the results. No dog copes better with being home alone as it ages if we do not do something about it. Dogs do not grow out of home alone problems. There is only one way to solve the problem—to teach the dog to be home alone! To accomplish this purpose we must follow a very precisely designed program.

Our experience with dogs and their owners show that the greater understanding the owner has for the mechanisms that have an impact on the dogs behavior in specific circumstances, the higher are the odds for changing the dog's behavior successfully. It is therefore of capital importance that the reader allows himself enough time to read and understand the next chapters in this book, before we proceed with the final treatment of CHAP.

Causes for CHAP

CHAP can have many causes:
1—lack of learning
2—unwillingness
3—understimulation
4—fear (anxiety)

We often see cases, where there are two or more causes for CHAP in one particular dog. Sometimes it is very difficult or impossible, to uncover the primary causes for CHAP.

Symptoms—destruction, endless howling sessions, soiling or total passivity (anxiety).

Lack of learning

We see the lack of learning to cope with being home alone primarily in puppies and young dogs, which normally call their pack members when left behind. They do that, as a rule, because they are understimulated or because they are fearful. They do that as a normal reaction to being alone. They call the pack, so to speak. These dogs have to learn to accept that sometimes they have to be alone. Prevention is better than cure, or in other words, better be safe than sorry. It is therefore important to teach the dog to be home alone, from the very first beginning.

Hidden symptoms

Adult dogs, suffering from CHAP, also show extremely positive reactions to treatment. In some cases, the CHAP disappears after one to two weeks.

11

These dogs have not learned to be home alone. The owners just left them home alone in periods and everything worked all right, more by luck than by understanding. When the problem arises, the owners then tell us that the dog could be home alone earlier—which is not right. The dog was not able to be home alone earlier, but the symptoms did not show clearly or not at all. The dog howled maybe a bit or even destroyed an old shoe or newspaper, but since they were not serious losses, the owner did not bother.

We must solve the problems as soon as they arise and that goes for CHAP as well. Whenever the dog shows the least symptom that loneliness disturbs it, commence immediately with the program that I describe in this book.

Unwillingness

We observe unwillingness, as a cause to CHAP, in dogs that live without rules, whenever the owners allow them to do precisely what they feel like doing, any time they want it. These dogs may sometimes howl or bark when the owners leave them alone for no more than a couple of minutes. They are not fearful; they have just been accustomed to get their will. The treatment for these dogs consists of a radical change in the daily co-existence between owner and dog. The owner must show the dog that it is him/her who makes decisions, and decides what, how, when and where, and not the dog. This does not imply that the owner suddenly becomes violent, brutal or indifferent, but rather consistent and purposeful.

The goal is to teach the dog to be able to conform to others. This is not a peculiar prerequisite—rather a necessity all animals can adhere. To live is definitely to adapt to the constantly unsteady environment. The problem with dogs is that, from puppyhood, owners too often give up and the dogs have it their own way. When we then find it

Wolves howl often when they cannot find the other pack members. Our dogs howl as well when they are alone. This is normal canine behavior. It does not help at all to reprimand the dog. To change the dog's behavior we simply have to teach it to be alone.

necessary to administrate rules, the dogs do not understand them. It is not because they do not want to—even if we call this problem unwillingness— but because they have not learned how.

Every dog owner has to teach his dog to understand and accept a *no* and to learn that its world does not fall into pieces just because of that. We will see, in chapter two, how to perform exercises to help the dog with these particular issues.

Understimulation is the most common cause for the dog to be destructive, even when dogs normally can be home alone without problems. These dogs do not show a genuine CHAP problem. If the dog

Understimulation

13

was not understimulated, it would have been able to be home alone without incidents. These dogs do not normally howl and bark; they just start their destruction derby whenever they feel like it. It is not, as I said, because they don't like to be home alone—they just have too much stored energy, which they can't get rid of besides being destructive. The cure is to activate the dog so that it does not have the need or the energy to *think* of being destructive or embark into such energy consuming pastimes.

Even if the lack of learning is the most common cause of CHAP, our experience shows that under-stimulation is the greatest single factor. Many dogs that we treat for CHAP show improvement as soon as the owners activate them. Some dogs have even shown improvement in spite of the owners executing the programs wrongly!

Separation anxiety

Dogs showing true separation anxiety are the most difficult to treat. Owners have a tendency to wait too long before they ask for advise or commence a treatment, which aggravates the problem.

Whenever the owner puts on his shoes or, for example, leaves the table after breakfast, the dog becomes anxious, or rather displays distress behavior, for the anxiety we cannot see. If it is anxiety, what their distress behaviour suggests, then these dogs are in a constant state of anxiety of being alone. Some dogs show more severe symptoms of anxiety than others and do not dare look away from the owners for a moment. Whenever the owner gets up, the dog follows him/her.

Some dogs follow their owners to the bathroom and they stand outside howling miserably if the owners have the audacity to shut the door. Dogs suffering from genuine separation anxiety howl and bark, urinate or defecate, or are destructive.

2. Don't do this!
—Old advise doesn't work

We have been studying dogs with CHAP for many years and have tried various methods, tricks and programs in our search for a solution to the problem. We know undoubtedly that some methods do not work and that others have a very limited effect. Pay attention to the following.

Toys

It does not help to give the dog toys whenever we left it alone. Some dogs do not notice the toys and others grab the toys for a short moment, but lose interest as soon as they find out that the owner is gone.

A second dog

It does not help to acquire one more dog. If you do that, the result is then, that you will have two dogs that can not be home alone. We often hear of unhappy dog owners advised to purchase a new dog as a companion for the existing dog. These owners began with one problem and ended up with two.

Dogs learn from one another, that is to say they have a tendency to imitate one another particularly in social activities. To howl is a social activity where imitation or contagion often happens. If you have one dog that howls when it is alone and you purchase a new dog, you will have, from one day to the next, two dogs that howl. Unwanted behavior seems to be more contagious than good manners.

Feeling guilty?

Only if the dog knows that it has done something wrong and that it remembers it, which is not the case.
Dogs that cannot be alone suffer and show it clearly through their body language. If the dog has had this problem for a long period, it will expect a negative reaction from the owner returning home. The dog therefore shows submission in order to pacify its angry owner. It is this submissive behavior, that we mistakenly interpret as feeling guilty. The dog has no idea whatsoever that it was wrong to chew a shoe 4 hours earlier.

Reprimanding

It all happens in the first 45 minutes

Reprimanding the dog has no effect since you can first accomplish that when you come home and you see the results of the dog's destructive activity. The dog cannot connect the scolding with its actions, which may have taken place several hours earlier. There is nothing to do when you come home to devastation and earthquakes-like indoor landscapes. Cleanup, have a soft drink, listen to a good record (a CD to the younger generation), watch TV, call a friend—in short, relax and take it as an experience! I know this is easier to say than to do, but at all costs do not let your frustration influence your good judgement. That will not help the dog, will not help you and only makes the problem more difficult to solve for you and your dog.

Most dogs howl, destroy things, urinate or defecate within the first 30 to 45 minutes after the owners leave them home alone. This is a tendency we have registered during our researches done 10 years ago. As soon as the owner left the dog, it became restless and began searching. Some dogs went berserk, jumping and running all over the place,

Very young puppies howl generally when by accident they get away from their siblings. They detest being alone because they need all the warmth to survive.

knocking everything off tables, including plants and expensive lamps—or furiously and energetically attacking the bookshelf, where many a good and cherished book ended up as trash.

Other dogs defecated on the floor, some on the couch, and yet others began their heartbroken howling choir. After the first 45 minutes, some of them calmed down for a while, but had spells of restlessness.

The second separation period

Most dogs tolerate the first loneliness period when you go to work, but not the second, as for example when you leave them in the evening. If you go out in the evening, you should activate your dog more than normal.

CHAP problems arise more often:

Holidays

After holidays — In our institute we have two particular periods, when we are very busy with an extraordinary number of CHAP cases—January and August, the after holidays periods. The dogs have then, for up to three weeks, been together

17

Nap time for puppies

Allow the puppy to be away from the owner during nap time. Encourage the puppy to go to its bed or crate, for example.

with their owners 24 hours a day. Suddenly one Monday morning life is back to normal—ours that is to say, not the dog's life. The dog cannot understand why it is now left alone—and now the trouble begins.

It is a good idea to train the dog to be alone everyday even when we are on holidays. It is not always necessary to take the dog to the beach, especially not in the middle of the day when the sun bakes.

The dog can also do without the shopping tour to the mall. Even those days when we stay home the whole day, we must designate some periods for the promotion of the dog's ability to cope with loneliness. If we are outdoors, the dog is in, and if we are indoors, the dog is out.

In other words, uphold the dogs abilities to be alone, to create its own entertaining opportunities. Do not create dependence, which subsequently will be difficult to eliminate.

Illness

We can expect CHAP whenever the owner has been ill. The owner has been at home for one week in close and constant contact with the dog and the day the owner returns to work, the dog feels the loneliness hard to withstand. During periods of illness, allow the dog to be alone in one room for several periods during the day. Do not allow the dog to follow you all over the place, as if it was your own shadow.

Guests

After periods with staying guests — Instruct the guests to allow the dog to be alone sometimes. The dog must not have attention all the time and must not get free treats at all. Do not encourage constant stroking and petting.

Working hours

After changing your work hours — Some dogs react very strongly to the owner's changing work hours. The only thing you can do is to teach the

This is a wonderful dog-bed that can easily be substituted when it gets too old. It is closed enough , yeilds good protection and it is cozy for the puppy.
A good dog-bed like this facilitates our work in teaching the dog to be home alone.

dog, through the daily interaction, to be as independent as possible; and of course activate it when you are at work.

It does not matter whether the owner activates the dog at five o'clock in the morning or at midnight.

The bedroom

Dogs that sleep in their owners' bedrooms are more prone to develop CHAP than dogs that sleep alone in their own beds—this was one of the conclusions in the research project we conducted.

Some dog owners find it cozy to have the dog in their bedroom. I do not wish to bring this issue into discussion, just remind my reader of the probable consequences. When the dog cannot be home alone during the night, in most cases it can neither be home alone during the day. Some dog owners in our research solved the CHAP in their dogs by literally banning the dog out from their bedrooms— and nothing else!

A wide program

It can be difficult to pinpoint the exact course of CHAP. Since the problem is so complex, I have developed a program, which we have used, with a satisfactory rate of success, for all types of CHAP.

The program consists of several points, which all contribute to the final result and I therefore advise dog owners not to omit some points, or select their favorite parts in the program.

The solution is to remove completely, or as much as possible, the causes of the problem, not only the symptoms. Sometimes it takes time, but after succeeding the results are generally lasting, only demanding a little maintenance.

Bongo after a hard day's work home alone!

3. The treatment of CHAP
—*On the treatment of the causes and not the symptoms*

Exercises in this chapter:
Combi-4
Searching
Tennis ball
Bed

Difficulty level:

The treatment of CHAP consists of several elements:

1. Contact exercises—Dogs suffering from CHAP seek a lot of contact. They usually assault guests with all possible and impossible expressions of joy. They are accustomed to getting all the contact they want whenever they want it. They have to learn that they will have the contact they need, but it is not free, and does not come when they desire it.

From the very first day we start the treatment of CHAP, the dog must not receive any free contact at all. The dog receives contact only when performing exercises.

Contact exercises

We teach the dog to do something in order to get something—to learn to earn! The first consequence of this program is an overall activation of the dog, especially the centers in its brain concerned with communication and social behavior. Secondly, we satisfy the dogs need of contact, e.g. petting and attention—it gets less, but more intense contact.

Nothing is free

Our goal is to have the dog come to a point where it would prefer not to have contact all the time. Contact has then become too stressful. When this happens we are seriously on our way to solve the problem with the dog's active co-operation.

The best exercise for this purpose is combi-4 (a combination of sit, stand, down, free). If both dog and owner can do better than that, they are welcome to perform a combi-5 (combi-4 plus come), or any other exercise focusing on the contact between owner and dog.

If you and your dog are not proficient with all

It does not matter which exercises you do with the dog or how correct you execute them. This is not an obedience competition! What you have to focus on is to allow the dog to work for the treats and the contact that it receives from you.

Searching

Problem solving

these exercises, you can hold off on combi-4 and work with combi-3 (sit, stand, free). I have even had a dog under treatment where we were forced to use combi-2 (sit, free) and a variation of combi-4 (Bongo, come, sit, free) in order to avoid conflicts between owner and dog and hereby worsening the problems.*

It does not really mater which combination you choose as long as you activate the dog and you cover its necessity of contact.

Execute contact exercises four to six times daily in periods of two to four minutes.

2. Searching — You can also activate those parts of the dog's brain concerned with olfactory impressions. The centers in the brain of the dog dealing with these impressions are extremely well developed. We must therefore give the dog daily searching exercises.

The easiest way to do this is to allow the dog to find its own food, preferably outdoors, irregardless of the weather, which is not an issue to most dogs. If the dog searches bits of food for 10 to 15 minutes, it will be well activated and presumably tired.

Do not worry with speculations about whether the dog eats bits of grass or dirt, when searching for food outdoors. There is no animal in nature that eats from clean and sterile bowls and they do not die from it.

You can give the dog searching exercises six to eight times daily. It is a good way to keep the dog occupied and it does not demand so much active co-operation from the owner. It is a good exercise for busy owners.

3. Problem solving is the ability to use previous experience in new combinations.

All animals solve problems and the dog is no exception. It has been selected throughout evolu-

The Combi-4 exercise or Sit, Stand, Down and Free—a simple exercise we can use to give the dog contact when it works for it. The signals must be given clearly with voice and hand movement. In the beginning you must always give the dog a treat immediately after it does what you want. Do not repeat the signals, be patient, give sound and hand signals simultaneously and remember Free when you finish. Ignore the dog after Free. Never give the dog a treat after you say 'free'.

Dogs are good at reading our facial expressions and body language. Always use clear signals. When the dog does what you want, give it a treat and a 'good' with an expression like the one shown here—it means friendliness in dog language.

tion for its ability to solve problems and we can expect it to have well-developed centers in the brain concerned with this activity. We can give them exercises by using a mug, a tennis ball, or something similar. This can be done by placing a couple of treats on the floor with an overturned mug covering them. Allow the dog to discover how to get the treats. This is an easy exercise for some dogs but a real puzzle for others.

It does not matter how long it takes the dog to solve the problem as long as it does not give up. Do not help the dog because then the dog will learn to give up easily. A helpless dog is very distressing and if, on top of that, it suffers from CHAP, then we are on a mission to solve the problem.

The tennis ball exercise is yet a variation of problem solving exercises. Cut a small hole in a tennis ball, fill it with treats and allow the dog to find out what to do.

The first exercises with the tennis ball must not be too difficult and the hole must therefore be big

Tennis ball exercise

The dog's bed (next page)

enough to allow the treats to come out easily. This will prevent the dog from beginning to chew the ball. With time and exercise the dog will master the art of getting treats out of tennis balls and you can cut very small holes in the balls making the exercise gradually more and more difficult.

You can execute this exercise as often as you wish and every time the dog needs activation. It is a good idea to leave some filled tennis balls in the house whenever you leave the dog alone.

4. The dog'd bed — The dog's bed plays a central role in the treatment of CHAP. We have to teach the dog to like it so that it tends to go and lay down in its bed rather than in any other place around the house. The idea is that whenever the dog is alone and it needs contact it would go to its bed since that is the place where it normally gets its need for contact satisfied. If the dog does that, we have won a lot. When the dog has laid down in its bed for a while and it is quiet and relaxed, it will, as a rule, fall asleep—and our problems are solved.

Periodically tell dog 'go to bed' and sit down a while by its side. Pet the dog and talk quietly to it. After a time just leave and ignore the dog, even if the dog follows you all over the place. We teach the dog that the bed means contact, it receives physical contact there and nowhere else and that it does not help at all to follow us.

Bear in mind that the dog's bed is not a punishment. Every single time the dog is in its bed we are nice and sympathetic.

You can give the dog this exercise as often as possible in the beginning. Uphold the meaning of the bed even after the dog has learned to be home alone.

Searching is tiring for the dog and it is therefore highly activating. Wolves are sometimes forced to search for food for a long period of time. Our dogs may also benefit from finding their food either indoors or outdoors inasmuch as they will thus be well activated.

5. The direct CHAP training — When all the preceding elements are ok, we can begin the direct treatment of the separation problem behavior. The

The direct CHAP training

25

The tennis ball exercise is good fun and very activating. A tennis ball is cheap and not noisy.

purpose of these exercises is to teach the dog to connect being alone with pleasure.

We move forward step-by-step. We have to be careful not to go forward to quickly. However be careful not to move forward to slowly. The steps in our program must remain connected to each other in a natural way and be perceived as such by the dog.

Read carefully the description of the program in the next chapter and look at the pictures, preferably several times. It is important the owner knows exactly what is happening at each step of the program and what the purpose is of that particular step.

A goal oriented program

This program is highly goal oriented and we have had great success with it—87 percent of all dogs we treat for CHAP show great improvement or total cure.

We will use a series of signals that the owner and the dog have to understand if we want to reach a successful outcome.

A dog that likes its bed is easier to leave home alone.

The bed must be connected with pleasure and always be regarded as a safe place. Give the dog contact, treats and pet it whenever it is in its bed the dog will quickly realize that the bed means safety.

It is very easy to understand how signals work once we understand the basic principles of signals and of all communication.

A signal is *everything* that means *something* to *someone*. When something means something to

27

What is a signal?

SMAF means Signal, Meaning And Form and is a way to describe signals accurately.

SMAF was first introduced by Roger Abrantes in his book in Danish 'Hunden, ulven ved din side' (Borgen Publishers 1994).

SMAF

Reinforcements

Whenever I write "!good" or "!treat" it means a reinforcement, i.e. everything that increases the rate at which the dog displays a certain behavior.

"!good" means that you say 'good' to your dog and "!treat" that you give the dog a treat.

someone his behavior changes and this is how we can see what our words, body postures, facial expressions and the likes mean for the dog.

Misunderstandings arise often between dog and owner because the owner believes that he is communicating a particular message to the dog and the dog understands it in a completely different manner. Whose fault? The owners to begin with. We have to be very sure and clear in our signals to the dog.

I describe signals in this book, as in all my books, in SMAF—an acronym that stands for Signal, Meaning And Form. SMAF is a way to describe signals as exactly as possible.

A signal is comprised of two parts: a meaning and a form.

Example: Bongo(look at me), sound(Booongo). In plain English, this means that I say 'Bongo' every time I want my dog to look at me.

Before the comma, we indicate then the meaning of the signal. *Bongo* is here the general name for the signal and it could be whatever we chose. *Look at me* is the meaning of the signal. After the comma, we indicate the form of the signal. *Sound* means that, in this specific signal, we use sound, a word for example, and between parenthesis we indicate the exact sound we use–*Booongo* in this specific case.

We write the whole sentence without any spaces to emphasize that the different parts comprise one single entity.

Signals without form are not signals, only thoughts; signals without meaning are neither signals, only noise.

Bongo(look at me),sound(Booongo)

The name of the signal	*The meaning of the signal*	*The form of the signal*	*The actual signal*

4. The dog learns to be alone

—*The direct treatment of CHAP*

Exercises in this chapter:
Direct CHAP training

Necessary signals to teach the dog to be home alone

The following signals are necessary to perform the exercises described as the direct treatment of CHAP. I describe all signals in SMAF (see page 28).

Difficulty level

Bongo(look at me),sound (Booongo)—the reader will of course not say Booongo unless his dog is called Bongo. Always pronounce Bongo the same way and with the same intonation. Do not use nicknames.

Bed(go to your bed),sound(bed)—say only bed and not go into your bed, good night, hasta la vista baby or whatever.

Bed,hand(point to the bed with your hand)—this signal supports Bed,sound.

No(stop now),sound(nooops)—use only the word *no* or even the sound *nooops* with a well emphasized and sizzling s-sound, which has been proven to have a good effect. Do not say 'stop that,' 'we don't want that,' or similar sentences that the dog cannot understand.

Find(find whatever),sound(find)—say only 'find'. The dog connects the sound *find* with using its nose and will find whatever is out there—in this specific case the food treats.

To teach the dog the signals we use, we have to motivate it.

The best possible motivation is the dog's necessity of food and contact. Healthy dogs, not least puppies and young dogs, are always ready to co-operate whenever they get something in return, be it food or contact. We use many food treats in the first steps off our learning processes. We do not need as many treats later on and in the end we only use treats to maintain certain learned patterns we wish to keep.

Exercise - Direct CHAP training

Plan of action (POA)

alt indicates an alternative POA in case the first POA doesn't work as we wanted it to.

Direct treatment of CHAP Level 1

1- Bongo,sound
2- Bed,sound + Bed,hand + Bed,treat = "!good"
3- Go 3-4 steps away from the dog. Place 2 treats on the floor and go back to the dog.
 alt3- The dog leaves the bed = No,sound.
 The dog returns to the bed = "!good"
4- Find,sound + Find,hand
5- The dog walks to the treats and eats them = do nothing, say nothing.
6- Start all over again from step 1. When performing step 3 walk farther and farther away from the dog.

This exercise is performed until the dog goes willingly to its bed and stays there calmly until the Find signal is given.

Send the dog to its bed with sound and hand signals. Use also Bed,treat which means that you've previously placed some treats in the bed.

Use "!good" which means saying the word while the dog is in its bed. If the dog tries t out of bed, say immediately no (No,sound) rememeber to use "!good" when the dog re to bed or stops the outgoing movement.

two treats on the floor, 3-4 feet from the
Keep an eye on the dog for it has to stay in
d.

Go back to the dog , wait a short moment and say
find *(Find,sound)*.

*Use the following signals and
reinforcements:*

1.

Bed,sound	**Bed,hand**	(!) "good"

2.

Find,sound	**Find,hand**	(!) "treat"

the dog to find the treats alone. Don't help the
The dog must learn how to solve problems without
lp of the owner.

Exercise -
Direct CHAP training

POA

Direct treatment of CHAP
Level 2

1- Bongo,sound
2- Bed,sound + Bed,hand + Bed,treat = "!good"
3- Leave the room where the dog is. Place 2 treats on the floor and go back to the dog.
  alt3- The dog leaves the bed = No,sound. The dog retyrns to the bed = "!good"
4- Find,sound + Find,hand
5- The dog walks to the treats and eats them = do nothing, say nothing.
6- Start all over again from step 1. When performing step 3 stay away for longer periods, but on an irregular schedule, e.g. 5 seconds, 15 seconds, 3 seconds.

This exercise is performed until the dog stays in its bed fully relaxed until the owner goes back and gives the find signal.

Place the treats farther away from the dog and in the general direction of the main entrance, or the entrance in the house that you normally use. The dog must remain calm and relaxed in its bed. before you proceed to the next level.

32

Direct treatment of CHAP
Level 3

1- Bongo,sound
2- Bed,sound + Bed,hand + Bed,treat = "!good"
3- Leave the room where the dog is and walk to the main door. Open and close the door twice as if you would go out and come in. Place 2 treats on the floor next to the main door and go back to the dog.
4- Find,sound
5- The dog walks to the treats and eats them = do nothing, say nothing.
6- Start all over again from step 1. When perform-ing step 3 wait for longer periods between the first open-close the door and the second. We simulate now that the dog is alone. Proceed on an irregular schedule, e.g. 5 seconds, 15 seconds, 3 seconds.
*   alt 6- The dog leaves the bed = No,sound.*
*   The dog howls = No,sound.*

This exercise is performed until the dog stays in its bed fully relaxed until the owner goes back and gives the find signal.

Exercise -
Direct CHAP training

POA

Now place the treats even farther away from the dog and preferably close to the main door. Remember always to go back to the dog before giving the signal find (Find,sound).

Exercise -
Direct CHAP training

POA

On level 4 we work with the main door, desensitizing it. We don't shut the door completely before several trials where we gradually close the door more and more. Wait a bit longer before coming back to the dog for every trial, though not on a regular schedule.

Direct treatment of CHAP
Level 4

1- Bongo,sound
2- Bed,sound + Bed,hand + Bed,treat = "!good"
3- Leave the room where the dog is and walk to the main door. Go out and stay out for 10-15 seconds. Place 2 treats on the floor next to the main door and go back to the dog.
4- Find,sound
5- The dog walks to the treats and eats them = do nothing, say nothing.
6- Start all over again from step 1. When performing step 3 stay out for longer periods. Proceed on an irregular schedule, e.g. 5 seconds, 2 minutes, 15 seconds, 10 minutes.
  alt 6- There are no alternative POA. If problems show up go back one level.

This exercise is performed until the dog remains fully relaxed whenever left alone, showing no signs of distress.

Results

You can expect to see positive results 8 to 10 days after you start this program provided everything works well and no time consuming problems show up at any level. However, you cannot expect to measure a consistently relaxed behavior in the dog, when left alone, before you have trained this program for three to four weeks.

How quick you will be able to measure results depends on many factors, such as the dog, the owner and the environment. The most important is that every owner/dog follow their own rhythm. For some dogs, it will take five days and for others a five-month period. A comparison has no purpose. Our goal is to teach the dog to be home alone—and that is the sole justification for our treatment. Our purpose is not to break records.

Be patient

Therefore be patient and understanding towards the dog's problem. We created the problem because we brought the dog to our homes and made the dog a family member, thereby removing it from what the dog originally was created.

Go back one level or two if necessary, until the dog shows no signs of any distress behavior, and continue then to the next levels of the program.

5. The daily routine
—Everything that is important when we do nothing important

No matter how experienced you are and how well you execute all the described exercises with your dog, you must assure your self that your daily routines do not work against your purposes, which unfortunately often is the case. Pay special attention to the following issues.

The bedroom Do not allow the dog to sleep in your or the kids' bedroom. If you succeed in teaching the dog to be alone during the night, you have built a good foundation to teach it to cope with being alone during the day.

Furniture Do not allow the dog to lay on couches or chairs. Dogs do that mostly to feel in touch with the owners, the couch with the owner's strong olfactory signature thus giving the dog a strong sense of the owner's presence. When the dog does not find its owner, it looks for relief in the safety given by the owner's smell. This is a very sweet thing for our animal friendly hearts and yet a disfavor we do our dogs by allowing them to do it. We are thus creating dependent beings that cannot deal with their environment on their own and CHAP is the clearest symptom of this. These over-dependent dogs must learn to find security in themselves. The bed—the dog's bed—is the ideal place to teach the dog independence. In the purpose built exercise, previously described, we teach the dog that its bed is safe. Hence, we teach the dog to be strong and to be able to rely on itself.

Free contact

Do not give the dog free contact particularly while the CHAP program is executed. If you give the dog free contact you undermine the very purpose of the contact exercises which consequently will not work properly. Why should the dog work to earn contact when it can get it free?

Contact on the owner's initiative

All contact with the dog must happen on the owner's initiative and not the dog's. You have to teach the dog how to satisfy its requirement for contact when you are present and not when the dog absolutely wants it. This is an important issue since it is one of the factors contributing to dogs not being able to be home alone.

Goodbye and welcome ceremonies

Do not perform any special farewell or welcome ceremony. The dog does not understand our lan-

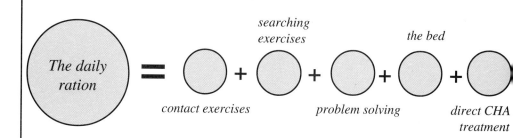

Dividing the dog's daily ration in portions for the purpose of training dogs to be able to be home alone

The daily ration = (contact exercises) + (searching exercises) + (problem solving) + (the bed) + (direct CHAP treatment)

guage and the only aim we achieve by doing that is to have the dog worrying about all the fuss. Upon leaving or returning home do it as routinely as possible, just as when you walk over to the kitchen from your living room to get a cup of coffee.

The main door and the keys

Touch frequently the knob of the main door, keys and all other items which the dog connects with being left alone. Open and close the main door, put your shoes on and take them off. You are hence desensitizing the dog to these items, which elicit the dog's distress of being alone.

Feeding

Feeding strategy—In order to achieve maximum effect, and since most of the exercises in the previous chapters demand the use of treats, you must use the dogs daily ration of food very strategically. Therefore every morning plan how you are going to feed your dog. You weigh the amount of food prescribed for your dog and divide it into different portions, each aiming at a group of specific exercises (see table).

When you have solved all your problems as well as the dog's problems, you must maintain the good behaviour patterns that you have taught our dog. Do not take the dog with you everywhere you go. Exercise home alone especially during holiday periods. Allow the dog to be home alone occasionally even if your work, private life or exceptional housing conditions make it viable and easy for you to take the dog with you wherever you go. CHAP has two common features with so many other behavior problems: it is much easier to prevent than to cure and it is much easier to create an unwanted behaviour pattern than to extinguish it.

In as much as understimulation, unwillingness, or lack of learning causes CHAP, the programs described in this book will certainly help dog owners to improve or completely remove the problem. If genuine anxiety causes the problem a solution often demands professional help. Search professional help preferably when the first symptoms show up. Our statistics show clearly that the younger the dog is, the easier it is to solve the problem.

Older dogs

Older dogs may find it especially difficult to be home alone and a solution is often very difficult or impossible. I therefore often recommend owners of older dogs to try to find a kind of babysitter solution to the problem. There are elderly in our community or neighborhood, wishing they could keep a dog that could keep them company and accompany them on a walk. These elderly often cannot cope with the work and especially with the idea of being solely responsible for the dog, but they make exceptional part-time dog owners. We have tried this solution with surprisingly good results. The elderly took care of the dogs during the day when the owners were at work and in the evening, the owners came back to fetch the dog and take it to its second (or first) home. The positive results were many: activated dogs, no soiled or destroyed homes, one and a half hours extra motion for both elderly and dogs. In addition—and perhaps the most important of all—more dogs were allowed to live, instead of being euthanized due to insurmountable problems.

The experiment shows us that we may have to learn to think untraditionally, to exploit unconventional ideas, to walk new paths and find new solutions. We may have to rethink our responsibility towards the creatures we enslaved and to forget for a moment our selfish motives.

The only difference between a good and a bad habit is that we like good habits and we do not like bad habits. Otherwise they are equally easy to create and equally difficult to extinguish.

PS – Psychopharmacology

We have witnessed in the '90s a great interest in the application of drugs in a variety of veterinary behavioral conditions. Groups have conducted studies into the clinical investigations of the use of buspirone, benzodiazepines, opioid antagonists, cloripramine and L-deprenyl in various veterinary behavioral conditions and among them CHAP (fear or anxiety).

It is not my purpose in the present context to give the reader a full account of the various products used for behavioral conditions. I will shortly mention the main products used by behavior veterinarians.

I also want to emphasize that I would only consider using psychopharmacology for CHAP whenever I can diagnose genuine fear or anxiety.

The clinical symptoms of anxiety are distress as the owner prepares to leave, following the owner like a shadow, strong vocalization like barking or howling in the first 45 minutes after the owner's departure, attempts to escape through doors or windows, destruction often around doors and windows, extreme salivation, passivity, urination and defecation.

Clinical symptoms of anxiety

We can also observe some of these symptoms where other factors cause the CHAP.

To cure CHAP, follow the program described in this book and remember to pay special attention to desensitization of the anxiety eliciting stimuli. Some behavior therapists use flooding, which can have a positive effect, however it is very difficult for the dog owner to apply appropriately.

Whenever you suspect that CHAP is caused by anxiety, you should let a veterinarian examine your dog. In some cases where we might suspect medical conditions I would recommend laboratory tests such as radiography, electroencephalography, a complete blood count, chemistry profile, thyroid panel and urianalysis.

In the past, behavior therapists prescribed phenothiazines and benzodiazepines for fear related cases including CHAP due to anxiety. None have proved fully satisfactory with many cases of relapse after a period. More recently, the tricyclic antidepressants and azapirones became increasingly popular.

In the table om page 43 I indicate the most common drugs used to alleviate fear. I want to emphasize strongly, that no drugs shall be used unless prescribed by the veterinarian. In the case of behavioral problems, and this applies also to CHAP, drugs should only be prescribed by a behavior veterinarian or a veterinarian in co-operation with a behavior therapist.

The results of the studies that we have conducted treating CHAP with drugs show, that drugs may help to speed up the process, but they do not solve the problem. In the cases where we have combined drugs with psychotherapy, we have obtained better results.

The bottom line is then, that the cure of CHAP must rely on a sensible psychotherapeutic program, in the modification of the daily patterns in the interaction between owner and dog and in a better understanding of canine behavior in general.

Drugs used to alleviate fear and anxiety

Drug class	Commonly used drug	Indication	Suggested canine dosage	Potential side effects	Contraindication	Onset of drug action
Azapirone	Buspirone (Buspar)	Generalized fear	2.5-10.0 mg PO bid per dog	Sedation, arousal	Potentiates diazepam	2–4 wks
Benzodiazepine	Diazepam (Valium)	Short-term sedation for fear	0.55 – 2.20 mg/kg PO prn	Sedation; increased seizure threshold; ataxia, muscle relaxation	Chronic fears and phobias; treatment requiring learning	Rapid
Beta-blocker	Propranolol (Inderal)	Mild manifestations of situational fears, or in combination with other anxiolytics, like buspirone	Propranolol, 5 – 40 mg PO tid per dog (depending on weight)	Urinary incontinence	Medical problems involving heart and circulation	Generally within 60 min after medication
Phenothiazine	Acepromazine maleate (Acepromazine)	Short-term sedation for fear	0.55 – 1.1 mg/kg PO; 0.055 – 0.110 mg/kg IM, SQ, IV	Sedation, agitation, reduced social and exploratory behavior	Chronic anxiety; animals showing paradoxical effects	Rapid (1–2 hrs)
Serotonin reuptake inhibitor	Fluoxetine (Prozac)	Chronic situational fears; conditions occurring in combination with other problems	1 mg/kg PO sid None	Decreased appetite, vomiting, restlessness	None	Approximately 4–6 wks
Tricyclic antidepressant	Amitriptyline (Elavil) Clomipramine (Anafranil)	Separation anxiety, chronic situational fears conditions occurring in combination with other problems	2.2 – 4.4 mg/kg PO bid 1 – 3 mg/kg PO sid	Sedation, dry mouth, constipation, urinary retention, cardiac conduction	Animals suffering from cardiac conditions or problems involving the urinary tract (especially infections)	After 4 wks

Source: Dodman, N.H. & Shuster, L. *Psychopharmacology of Animal Behavior Disorders* (Blackwell Science Inc. 1998)

6. Bongo home alone

—There's no limit for what one can do for his humans.

Story by Daniel and Roger Abrantes
Illustrations by Henriette Westh
From the book 'Hunden – ulven ved din side'
Borgen Publishers © 1994

Index

A

activate   17
a wide program   19

B

bed   19, 25

C

changing work hours   18
CHAP   10
contact exercises   21
couches   37

D

desensitizing   39
direct treatment   25, 30
distress behavior   36
door   39

F

feeding   39
free contact   38

G

guests   18

H

holidays   17

I

illness   18

L

lack of learning   11

M

misunderstanding   28

N

new dog   15

O

older dogs   40

P

problem solving   22, 24
psychopharmacology 41, 42, 43

R

reprimanding   16
results   36

S

searching   22
separation anxiety   14
signal   28
sleeping room   19
SMAF   28
statistics   10
symptoms   40

T

tennis ball exercise   24
toys   15

U

understimulation   13, 39
unwillingness   12

Some litterature for further reading

Abrantes, R.A., (1993) - The Develpoment of Social Behaviour (in The Behaviour of Dogs and Cats, by members of the APBC).
Abrantes, R.A., (1994) - The Art and Science of Communication (in Transcript of Waltham APBC Symposiun 1994).
Abrantes, R.A., (1997) - Hunden alene hjemme.
Abrantes, R.A.,(1997) - The Evolution of Canine Social Behaviour.

Borchelt, P.L., & Voith, V. (1982) - Treatment and Diagnosis of Separation Anxiety Problems.

Christiansen, F.W & Rothausen, B., (1983) - Behaviour Patterns Inside and Around the Den of a Captive Wolf Pack.

Dodman, N.H. & Shuster, L. (1998) - Psychopharmacology of Animal Behavior Disorders

Fox, M.W., (1968) - Abnormal Behavior in Animals.

Holland, J.G., Skinner, B.F., (1961) - The Analysis of Behavior.

Joby, R., Jemmett, J.E., Miller, A.S.H., (1984) - The control of undesirable behaviour in male dogs using megestrol acetate.

McConnell, P. (1998) The Cautious Canine—How to Help Dogs Conquer Their Fears.
Mertens, P., Doodman, N.H. &Unshelm J., (1996) - Separation Anxiety—Pharmacological treatment of a Yuppie-puppy Syndrome.
Mugford, R.A., (1982) - Behaviour Problems in the Dog.

Voith, V.L., (1982) - Possible Pharmacological Approaches to Treating Behavioral Problems in Animals.
Voith, V.L. & Borchelt, P.L., (1985) - Separation Anxiety in Dogs
Voith, V.L. & Borchelt, P.L., (1985) - Fears and Phobias in Companion Animals.
Scott, J.P. & Fuller J.L., (1965) - Genetics and Social Behavior of the Dog
Seligman, E.P., (1975) - Helplessness.

The Evolution Of Social Canine Behaviour

by Roger Abrantes

This book is a detailed study of the evolution of canine social behaviour. The author leads the reader, step by step, through the various aspects involved in the development of single social behaviour patterns. This book is also a comparative study, where the reader is lead from one argument to the next with mathematical precision.

A surprising book, dismissing common believes and assumptions, and leaving the reader with simple sound explanations. A book for all students of animal behaviour, as well as for all readers fascinated by animal behaviour wishing to uncover the whys and hows of canine social behaviour.

'The idea of dominance-aggression is biased. It is possible to be aggressive and dominant, but the term suggests the dog attacks because it is dominant. No dog attacks because of dominance. Dominance aims at controlling another by means of ritualised behaviour, without harming or injuring it. The final attack, if there is one, is motivated by aggression alone.

Saying that a dog is a fear-biter, is equivalent to saying that the dog does not behave purposefully. By saying that the dog shows submissive-aggression we simultaneously answer the question of how to solve the problem. The dog is submissive, which means reacting to a threat by another, giving in, and surrendering. It only becomes aggressive because its behaviour does not have the desired effect. The dog is then under threat and ready to react by flight or immobility. If flight is not possible, it may freeze. Some do and die. Others resort to their last defense, they attack, and then the drive of aggression takes over. This situation is easily avoided by accepting the dog's submission or allowing it to flee.

Dog Language

An Encyclopedia Of Canine Behaviour
by Roger Abrantes

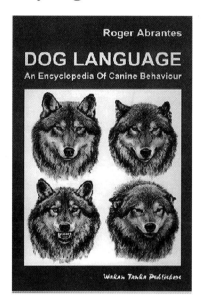

Dog Language tells us why dogs do what they do and how we can express ourselves so that our dogs understand us better. It is a systematic book, ordered alphabetically with 293 entries and 94 beautiful drawings illustrating over 150 different dog expressions.

First published in Scandinavia in 1986 as *'Hundesprog'*, this book became a great success and has since then helped many thousands of dog owners, instructors, behaviour students and veterinarians to understand dogs. Now available in English, the present edition of *Dog Language* is an updated, highly revised and enlarged version of the original *'Hundesprog'*.

Following the traditions of the school of ethology founded by Konrad Lorenz, *Dog Language* is based on many hours of research, observation and study. *Dog Language* is a no-nonsense book, written in a modern and uncomplicated style—a book for all readers with interest in dogs, wolves and other canids.

Roger Abrantes, ethologist, PhD, DHC, MAPBC, is the author to 17 books published in Danish, Swedish, Norwegian and English. He is currently the scientific director of the Institute of Ethology at the Høng Agriculture School, Denmark.

RA has participated in many TV and radio programmes all over the world. He has been adviser for the Danish Police Force, Technologic Institute, the Icelandic Kennel Club and guest lecturer at the Danish Veterinary University. He is a very demanded speaker at international symposiums in Europe and America. He often guest lectures at several universities, including the University of Illinois in the USA.

You can order books by calling or writting to

Wakan Tanka Publishers

11 South 706, Lillian Court, Naperville, Il. 60564, USA
Phone (+1) 630 904 0896 — Telefax 630 904 7987
E-mail <wtanka@aol.com>
http://users.aol.com/jemeyers/wt.htm

Wakan Tanka Seminars

arranges talks and seminars with the author of this book. Please call for more information.

You can also contact the author of this book at
<roger@abrantes.com>

Association Of Pet Behaviour Councellors
PO Box 46, Worcester, WR8 9YS, England

Tel/Fax + 44 1386 751151
E-mail <apbc@petbcent.demon.co.uk
http://webzone1.co.uk/www/apbc